ZOO ANIMALS
IN THE WILD

PARROT

JINNY JOHNSON

ILLUSTRATED BY MICHAEL WOODS

W

FRANKLIN WATTS
LONDON • SYDNEY

An Appleseed Editions book

First published in 2006 by Franklin Watts
338 Euston Road, London NW1 3BH

Franklin Watts Australia
Hachette Children's Books
Level 17/207 Kent St, Sydney, NSW 2000

© 2006 Appleseed Editions

Created by Appleseed Editions Ltd, Well House,
Friars Hill, Guestling, East Sussex TN35 4ET

Designed by Helen James
Edited by Mary-Jane Wilkins
Illustrated by Michael Woods

ISBN 0 7496 6731 1

Dewey Classification: 598.7`1

A CIP catalogue for this book is available from the British Library

Photographs by Alamy (Juniors Bildarchiv, Humberto Olarte Cupas, Martin Harvey,
Christian Kapteyn, Kees Metselaar, Natural Visions, Steve Bloom Images, Genevieve Vallee,
David Wall), Getty Images (Theo Allofs, Sylvain Grandadam, Kim Heacox, Johner,
Timothy Laman, Joel Sartore, Kevin Schafer)

Printed and bound in Thailand

Contents

Parrots

Everyone knows what a parrot looks like. This brightly-coloured bird has a big hooked beak and lives in jungle trees. It squawks noisily as it flies from branch to branch.

The scarlet macaw is a large parrot which lives in Central and South American jungles.

In fact, there are lots of different kinds of parrots. Most are colourful, but some have dull green, grey or black feathers. Many do live in the jungle, but there are parrots in cooler, drier places too, and some spend most of their time on the ground. There is even a parrot in New Zealand called the kakapo, which can't fly!

The African grey parrot is very good at copying human speech.

The kea is the only parrot that lives on mountains.

The parrot family

There are more than 350 different kinds of bird in the parrot family. They have different names, such as parakeets, cockatoos, macaws, conures, lories and lorikeets, lovebirds and budgerigars.

Male

Female

Many male and female parrots look the same, but the male eclectus parrot is green, while the female is red and blue.

Many different kinds of parrot live in zoos. Some of the most popular are cockatoos, scarlet macaws, hyacinthine macaws (shown here) and blue-crowned parrots.

The biggest parrot is the hyacinthine macaw, which is more than a metre long. Littlest are the pygmy parrots – even smaller than budgerigars.

All parrots have short legs and strong feet with four toes. Two toes face forwards and two backwards, so the parrot can grip branches strongly.

Budgerigars are some of the smallest parrots.

A parrot's beak

A parrot's beak is strong enough to crush hard seeds and nuts. The big, curving top half fits over the smaller, shorter lower half. Above the beak is a bulgy area called the cere, where the parrot's nostrils are.

A parrot's beak is shaped to suit the food it eats. Macaws have the biggest, strongest beaks.

A parrot's beak keeps growing all through its life and the bird has to chew on branches to stop its beak getting too long.

A parrot's tongue is fleshy and strong. It uses it to hold on to things and to work out the tasty parts of nuts and fruits.

The long-billed corella uses its long beak to dig for food such as roots and bulbs.

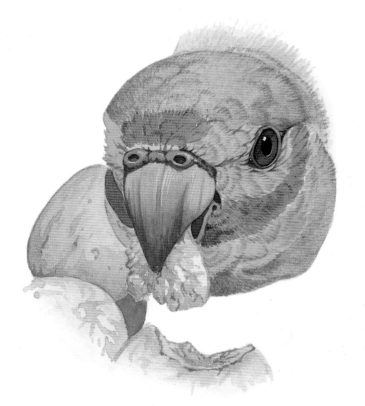

The fig parrot feeds mainly on the tiny seeds in figs, picking them out of the fruit with its slender beak.

At home in the wild

Parrots generally live in warm parts of the world. The places with the most different types of parrot are Australia and the Amazon rainforest in South America. Parrots also live in Central America, Africa, Southeast Asia and New Zealand.

A parrot needs trees or other places where it can perch, sleep and feed, and it must be able to find fresh water. Tropical rainforests are a favourite home for many kinds of parrot, but some parrots live in open country too.

Cockatoos live all over Australia, even in dry areas and grassland.

There are 17 different kinds of macaw in the Central and South American rainforests.

At home in the zoo

Good zoos keep parrots in large enclosures called aviaries rather than in cages. They try to make the aviaries as much like the parrots' home in the wild as possible, with plenty of plants and places to perch.

Zoos also give their parrots an indoor area where they can get away from zoo visitors and sleep at night. This area is heated in winter as most parrots are used to tropical warmth and don't

Zoo parrots like lots of perches at different heights in their enclosure.

Blue and gold macaws are very rare in the wild.

like the cold. Parrots are very clever birds. To stop them becoming bored in the zoo, their keepers give them plenty of things to play with, as well as branches to gnaw on.

Searching for a treat in an old cardboard box is fun for a zoo parrot.

On the move

Parrots are expert climbers. They can grip firmly with their feet and use their beaks like a third foot to hold on when clambering from branch to branch.

All parrots can fly, except the kakapo. Fast fliers usually have long, narrow wings and a long tail. Macaws can fly at 50 kilometres an hour – as fast as a car driving in a city street.

Other parrots have broader, blunter wings and shorter tails and they fly more slowly.

A scarlet macaw with outstretched wings.

A red and green macaw uses its beak to help it climb from branch to branch.

A parrot's day

Parrots usually sleep in big groups in the trees, each on a favourite perch. At sunrise, the birds wake up and fly off in groups to find food with much screeching and squawking.

The parrots spend the morning feeding, while a few of the flock keep watch. They call loudly to warn the others if any predators (such as hawks) come near. Then the whole flock flies up into the air. In the middle of the day the parrots take a break to rest and clean their feathers.

A pair of red and green macaws in flight.

Many wild parrots like to take a rain bath – when it rains they hang upside down with their wings spread until their feathers are thoroughly wet. Many zoos provide a sprinkler system so their parrots can enjoy a bath too.

The parrots start feeding again late in the afternoon. As sunset comes the parrots fly back to their roosting tree and settle down for the night.

Some macaws lick clay on river banks. The clay may help to protect the birds from poisonous chemicals in some seeds they eat.

Feeding

Fruit, seeds and nuts are parrots' favourite foods. They can crack the hardest shells, such as brazil nuts, with their powerful beaks. Some parrots also eat insects.

This macaw is holding a nut with one foot while it breaks it open with its strong beak.

Lories and lorikeets prefer softer foods. They have a long tongue tipped with a tuft-like fringe, which they use to collect pollen and nectar from flowers.

The rainbow lorikeet feeds on eucalyptus flowers. It crushes the flowers with its beak, then soaks up the nectar and pollen with its special brush-tipped tongue.

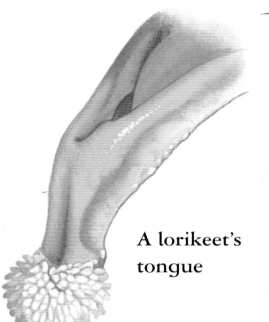

A lorikeet's tongue

Zoo parrots are fed plenty of seed and grain, as well as lots of fresh fruit and vegetables such as greens, carrots and mango. They are given special treats, too, such as grapes.

Family life

Parrots like company. Male and female pairs may stay together for many years and parrots often gather in huge flocks of hundreds of birds.

Parrot pairs help to keep each other's feathers clean. This is called preening. The birds nibble and chew the feathers to remove dirt. Many parrots have special feathers which have edges

A flock of rose-breasted cockatoos takes to the air.

that break into a powder. The parrots use this powder to clean the rest of their feathers.

A pair of black-capped lories preening their feathers.

Zoos sometimes keep different kinds of parrots together. All the birds need to be about the same size otherwise the larger birds may attack the smaller ones.

Nesting time

Parrots lay eggs once or twice a year.
The female bird and her mate find a nest,
which is usually a hole in a tree trunk or
a cliff. They may dig out the hole with
their beaks to make it bigger.

A male blue-winged parrot
brings food to his mate as she
sits on their eggs in a hollow tree.

Zoo parrots have nesting boxes where they can lay their eggs and keep them warm.

This macaw has found a tree hole that might make a perfect nest site.

Large parrots lay between one and three eggs. Smaller birds may lay as many as six eggs. The female incubates the eggs – keeps them warm – for 18 to 30 days until they are ready to hatch. The male bird may help, but usually he brings his mate food while she stays on the nest.

Hatching

When baby parrots first hatch, they are blind and helpless. For the first week, the father flies off and brings back food for the whole family. The mother stays to guard the tiny chicks.

As the chicks grow bigger they need more to eat, so the mother bird also leaves them to gather food with the father.

Baby parrots grow quickly and their eyes open a couple of weeks after hatching.

The chicks can't start learning to fly until they have all their feathers. Large parrots take three or four months to grow them all.

Young parrots stay with their parents for a year or more. Parrots can live to be 70 years old.

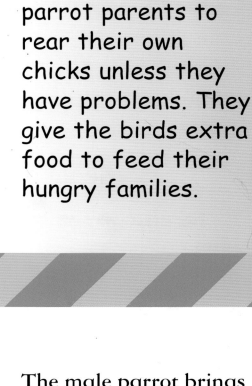

Keepers leave parrot parents to rear their own chicks unless they have problems. They give the birds extra food to feed their hungry families.

The male parrot brings food for the mother and young at first. When the chicks are big enough to leave, the mother helps her mate gather food for them.

Keeping in touch

Parrots are very noisy and constantly squawk and call to each other as they fly and feed.

One of the loudest parrot calls is a screeching alarm call, which can travel a long way. But parrots do make some gentler whistling, twittering sounds as well.

The blue-fronted Amazon is a popular pet because it is so good at mimicking human speech.

A palm cockatoo drums on a branch with a stick.

The palm cockatoo makes a special sound when it defends its nest site. It holds a stick in its beak and drums noisily on a branch with it to warn off intruders.

Pet and zoo parrots imitate human voices. The African grey parrot and the blue-fronted Amazon are two of the best talkers.

Parrot fact file

Here is some more information about parrots. Your mum or dad might like to read this, or you could read these pages together.

A parrot is a bird. There are about 352 species, or kinds, of parrots with many different names. Main groups include parrots, macaws, amazons, conures, parakeets, parrotlets, cockatoos, pygmy parrots and fig parrots, lovebirds, lories, lorikeets and budgerigars.

Where parrots live

Most parrots live in the southern half of the world. There are parrots in Central and South America, Africa, southern Asia, Australia and New Zealand.

Parrot numbers

More than a quarter of parrot species are very rare, and some are close to becoming extinct. Many of these are rare because large areas of their forest homes have been destroyed and because people capture birds illegally for sale as pets. The hyacinthine macaw is one of the parrots in danger of disappearing from the wild. There may be only about 3000 wild birds left.

Size

The biggest parrot is the hyacinthine macaw, which is about
1 metre long. Smallest are the pygmy parrots from New Guinea,
which are only 9 centimetres long.

Find out more

If you want to know more about parrots, check out these websites.

San Diego Zoo
http://www.sandiegozoo.org/animalbytes/t-macaw.html

Smithsonian National Zoo
http://nationalzoo.si.edu/Animals/Birds/Facts/FactSheets/
fact-palmcockatoo.cfm

BBC Science and Nature
http://www.bbc.co.uk/nature/animals
/pets/parrots.shtml

Animal Diversity Web
http://animaldiversity.ummz.umich.
edu/site/accounts/pictures/psittacidae

Words to remember

aviary
A large cage built specially for birds.

enclosure
The area where an animal or bird lives in a zoo.

eucalyptus
A kind of tree that grows in Australia.

extinct
An animal becomes extinct when there are no more left in the wild.

incubate
To keep eggs warm until they hatch.

jungle
Another name for rainforest.

mate
Male and female parrots pair up to lay eggs and care for young. A parrot's partner is called its mate.

nectar
Sugary liquid made by flowers which some birds feed on.

pollen
Powdery substance inside flowers.

predator
An animal that lives by hunting and killing other animals.

rainforest
Forests that grow in very hot, wet places in tropical parts of the world.

roost
To rest or sleep on a perch or branch.

Index